LITTLE
WORLD RELIGIONS

Published in the United States by Viva Editions, an imprint of Start Midnight,
LLC, 221 River Street, Ninth Floor, Hoboken, New Jersey 07030.

Printed in the United States

10 9 8 7 6 5 4 3 2 1

Trade paper ISBN: 978-1-63228-087-9

E-book ISBN: 978-1-63228-144-9

The
LITTLE BOOK OF
WORLD RELIGIONS

Ross Dickinson

VIVA
EDITIONS

Contents

Introduction

The impact of religion on our world is colossal. Whether you are Jewish or Christian, Muslim or Hindu, whether you are devoutly pious or occasionally spiritual or curiously agnostic or firmly atheistic, religion is woven into the fabric of all our lives. In its myriad shapes and forms, in both its presence and its absence, it can divide people as much as it can bring them together. It can unite dinner tables and countries and even entire empires, or it can drive a wedge between those same dinner tables, those same countries, those same empires. Yet the fact that religion is *here*, right now and all around us, and the fact that it has been for a very long time and will doubtlessly continue as such into the future, is as fundamental to the understanding of the human condition as language, music and cooked food.

Religion is absolutely enormous. Its history. Its weight. Its sheer variety. With this in mind, *The Little Book of World Religions* is, as the name suggests, only a "beginners" guide to the basics. What you are holding in your hands is not an exhaustive academic text but, rather, a whistle-stop tour of the world's major religions (and several of its minor ones). Here you will find the key facts, beliefs and histories of the faiths followed by a vast proportion of the world's population, as well as a range of surprising stories, colorful characters and nuggets of information that will leave you aching to find out more. Together, we'll explore the Big Five (Judaism, Christianity, Islam, Hinduism and Buddhism) before immersing ourselves in less well-known (but no less important) faiths such as Zoroastrianism, Shinto, Voodoo and Rastafarianism. But, before all that, let's go back as far as we can to the earliest known days of religion, when ancient belief systems dominated the cultures and lives of millions.

ANCIENT
RELIGIONS

The word "religion" comes from the Latin *religare* (meaning "to bind fast"), so we could argue that before the Romans there was no such thing as religion, for the word had not yet been invented. But that's obviously silly—we know that the Greeks had their own pantheon of gods and goddesses long before the Romans, and that the Ancient Egyptians had theirs long before even the Greeks. Maybe, *technically*, these were mythologies rather than religions. They certainly had some staggering differences to the religions of the modern world (foremost among them, in some cases, the sacrifice of animals and even people). Yet they also had many similarities to the doctrines which continue to be practiced today: deities, rituals, places of worship, notions of the afterlife, priests and prayer. They may be extinct in the twenty-first century, but these religions of old certainly helped pave the way for the many faiths which followed them.

Mesopotamian

Mesopotamia is one of the oldest known civilizations in the world, and it gave us one of the oldest known mythologies, with written records of religious practices in the area dating as far back as 3500 BC. Mesopotamia itself—the land "between two rivers," the Tigris and the Euphrates—was largely what we now call Iraq, and its pantheon of gods all came from two original deities who emerged from the swirling waters of Creation: the male Apsu from fresh water and the female Tiamat from salt water. From these two, thousands of gods came into being, the most important of which were Anu (ruler of heaven), Ki (ruler of earth), Enlil (ruler of air) and Enki (ruler of sea). Despite its astonishingly old origins, the mythology of Mesopotamia includes several tales and legends which will be instantly recognizable to most readers. The *Atrahasis*, for example, is the epic of a great flood sent by the gods to destroy all human life except for that of Atrahasis himself—a wise man who survives the deluge after the gods tell him to build a boat.

Ancient Egyptian

Around 3100 BC, several centuries after Mesopotamian mythologies arose, Egypt was unified, remaining as one of the most powerful civilizations in the world until it was conquered by Alexander the Great in 332 BC. Ancient Egypt is famous today for its towering pyramids and its once-mysterious system of hieroglyphs, and the names of many of its gods and goddesses remain well known to this day. There's the lord of the underworld, Osiris, and his lover (and sister), the mother goddess Isis. There's Ra, the god of the sun, and the jackal-headed god of death, Anubis. The goddess of cats was Bast—cats featured heavily in Ancient Egyptian mythology, as they were believed to be sacred or even deities themselves—and she was also the goddess of sex and fertility. Geb was the god of the earth and his wife, Nut, the goddess of the sky. These latter two are perhaps the most beautifully depicted of all the Egyptian gods—Geb's skin is covered by hills, rivers and forests; Nut's by constellations of stars.

Ancient Greek

The Ancient Greeks were keen storytellers, and it was in the godly realm that their stories were perhaps the most magnificent. Theirs was a polytheistic mythology, with the 12 Olympians (so named because they lived on Mount Olympus) considered to be the principal gods and goddesses. The king of the Olympian gods was Zeus who, though married to Hera, had a penchant for seducing and sometimes impregnating other goddesses, mortal women, and even the occasional female animal. God of the sea was Poseidon, goddess of love was Aphrodite and god of war was Ares.

But the Olympians were not the only deities for the Ancient Greeks. In fact, there were multitudes. Another race of gods were the Titans—among them Prometheus, who stole fire from the gods to give to mankind. He was punished for his treachery by being chained to a rock, where each day an eagle ate his liver, and each night his liver grew back again to be eaten once more the following day. And there was Atlas, who was made to bear the weight of the heavens on his shoulders—again as a punishment, because he led the Titan gods in their battle against Zeus' Olympian gods.

These myriad gods were worshipped in myriad ways by the Ancient Greeks. Sacrifices regularly took place with the slaughtering of animals, but other, simpler sacrifices were also common—families would often not eat and therefore "sacrifice" a portion of their evening meal for Hestia, the goddess of the hearth. Many of the famous buildings from Ancient Greek times were erected as a form of worship: the Parthenon for the goddess Athena (the patron deity of Athens); the Temple of Apollo in Delphi (also the seat of the Oracle of Delphi—a priestess who could be consulted for prophecies said to come from Apollo himself); the Temple of Zeus in Olympia (home to one of the Seven Wonders of the Ancient World, the statue of Zeus). Even the original Olympic Games, held in Olympia under the shadow of the Temple of Zeus, were a festival for and form of worship of Zeus.

Roman

There are many similarities between the Ancient Greek pantheon and the Roman. The Greek Zeus was the Roman Jupiter. The Greek goddess of marriage was Hera and her Roman counterpart was Juno. Both had gods of wine: Dionysus in Greece and Bacchus in the Roman Empire. That they were so similar is of little surprise—both civilizations existed largely across the same eras, separated only by the narrow Adriatic and Ionian Seas, and the Romans adopted many ideas and stories from the Greeks.

Though there aren't quite so many similarities between the polytheism of the Romans and the monotheism of the three Abrahamic religions (Judaism, Christianity and Islam) which dominate the world today, the Roman Empire's pantheon of gods nevertheless had a profound impact upon the modern world. Many of its celestial beings gave their names to the celestial bodies which comprise our solar system—among them, the aforementioned Jupiter, as well as Mercury (god of trade), Venus (goddess of love), Mars (god of war) and Neptune (god of the sea). Likewise, Christianity was able to establish and spread itself more widely because it was adopted as the state religion of the Roman Empire some three centuries after the death of Jesus.

Aztec

On the other side of the Atlantic Ocean, we can find another remarkable empire with its own unique set of religious beliefs. Though it developed much later than the other religions so far discussed (the civilization coalesced sometime in the fourteenth century and lasted until the Spanish conquest in the sixteenth), the Aztec Empire nevertheless engaged in practices we think of today as ancient—most notably that of human sacrifice. It was believed that this particular form of worship must occur daily, for without the blood of a human sacrifice the sun would not rise in the morning. Aztec mythology is resplendent with gods and goddesses whose depictions are as colorful as their names are difficult to pronounce. Among them are Huītzilōpōchtli ("left-handed hummingbird"), the god of war; Quetzalcoatl ("feathered serpent"), the god of life; Tezcatlipoca ("smoking mirror"), the god of the night; and Chicomecōātl ("seven snakes"), the goddess of agriculture.

Norse

The grand stories of Norse mythology, complete with Valkyries, trolls, epic battles and all-powerful hammers, were the creation of the Vikings in Scandinavia in *c.*790–1100 CE. Traces of these stories and characters can still be found in the various belief systems of Modern Paganism, as well as in countless comic books and blockbuster movies. At the head of the Norse gods is Odin: supreme deity, king, one-armed shape-shifter, husband to Frigg (goddess and queen) and father to, among many others, the contrary brothers Thor (god of thunder) and Loki (god of mischief). The land of the gods, Asgard, is one of nine worlds (the world of man is called Midgard) which are all connected by the great tree Ygdrasil.

THE BIG FIVE

The Big Five are the world's principal religions—in alphabetical order: Buddhism, Christianity, Hinduism, Islam and Judaism. Yet the order in which you will find them in this book is not alphabetical. Nor is it an order of supposed importance. Instead, the three Abrahamic faiths (Judaism, Christianity and Islam, which descend from the teachings of the prophet Abraham) will come first in their own chronological order, followed by the two Eastern faiths in the same manner. Known as the Big Five thanks to the enormous number of followers they have across the world (together, they comprise almost five billion people), these are the most widespread and well-known religions on the planet today. And, while the Abrahamic and the Eastern faiths share more in common with themselves than with each other, there are similarities which extend across all five. Most notable among these is what is known as the Golden Rule—that we should treat others as we wish to be treated.

Judaism

ORIGIN: 2000—1800 BC, Canaan
(modern-day Israel/Palestine)

DEITY: Yahweh

SYMBOLS: Star of David; Menorah

KEY SCRIPTURES: Torah; Talmud; Tanakh

MAJOR FIGURES: Abraham; Moses; David

KEY FESTIVALS AND HOLY DAYS: Passover, March/
April (celebration of the Exodus); Yom Kippur,
September/October (the Day of Atonement);
Hanukkah, December (Festival of Lights)

NOTABLE BRANCHES: Orthodox; Conservative; Reform

ESTIMATED ADHERENTS: 14 million (0.18 percent
of world population)

Judaism was the first major monotheistic faith, and few other religions have a history as rich, and as tortured. That there are only 14 million Jewish people in the world today (there are almost twice as many Sikhs) is perhaps not all that surprising when we consider the struggles their antecedents were forced to endure—among them, slavery and the Holocaust. Yet the resilience and the devotion of the Jewish community continues, just as it has done for almost 4,000 years, making Judaism one of the oldest extant religions in the world.

BELIEFS

In the late 1100s, the Jewish scholar Maimonides (also known as Rambam) sought to summarize the core tenets of the religion in his 13 Principles of Faith, which can be found in his 14-book-long Mishneh Torah. These principles, which focus mostly on Yahweh (the Hebrew word for God), are widely accepted as the fundamental beliefs of Judaism.

1. God exists.
2. There is only one God.
3. God is incorporeal.
4. God is eternal.
5. Prayer is to be directed to God and not to other, false gods.
6. The words of the prophets are true.
7. The prophecies of Moses are primary.
8. The origin of the Torah is divine.
9. The Torah cannot be changed.
10. God is omniscient (all-knowing).
11. God will reward those who follow his commandments and punish those who transgress them.
12. The Messiah will arrive.
13. The dead will be resurrected.

THE GOLDEN RULE IN JUDAISM

"You shall not take vengeance or bear a grudge against your kinsfolk. Love your neighbor as yourself."— Leviticus 19:18

EARLY HISTORY: ABRAHAM

According to the Seventh Principle of Faith, Moses is the true prophet of Judaism. And yet Jewish history and heritage actually stretches back even further than Moses— by perhaps another 500 years—to Abraham. He and his wife Sarah were an old and childless Hebrew couple when God chose him to establish a covenant: in exchange for Abraham's devotion and his teaching of others that God was the one and the only, Abraham would be blessed with many children and with sacred land in Canaan (modern-day Israel/Palestine). It was Abraham's grandson, Jacob, who first took the name Israel, and from then on Abraham's descendants, the chosen people, were known as Israelites.

EARLY HISTORY: MOSES

In the years between Abraham and Moses, many of the Israelites migrated to Egypt, where they were enslaved by the ruling Pharaoh. The oppression did not stop there. In an effort to curtail the Israelite population, the Egyptian Pharaoh, fearing that they might rise up and compete with his power, ordered all newborn male Hebrew children to be drowned in the River Nile. A Hebrew woman called Jochebed sought to save her baby by hiding him in a basket in a patch of riverside bulrushes. The baby was found by none other than the Pharaoh's daughter, who rescued him, adopted him as her own and gave him the name Moses. Thus, Moses grew up as an Egyptian prince.

Despite his royal status, Moses developed a sympathy for the Hebrew slaves, and when, as an adult, he witnessed an Egyptian beating a Hebrew, Moses killed the Egyptian, fleeing into the desert immediately after and finding work as a shepherd. It was here that he first heard the voice of God (from a flaming bush) commanding him to return to Egypt and lead his people out of slavery and into the promised land. Moses attempted to do so but the Pharaoh refused to emancipate the slaves, and so God wrought ten plagues upon the Egyptians, at the culmination of which the Pharaoh finally allowed Moses to lead the Hebrews out of Egypt.

Nevertheless, the Pharaoh did not keep his word, sending his army to recapture the liberated slaves. On the shores of the Red Sea, defeat seemed inevitable, until Moses parted the waters and led the Hebrews across to safety. When the Egyptian army followed, the Red Sea closed in upon them, killing them all. Upon reaching Mount Sinai, Moses climbed the mountain, where God came to him once more, re-establishing the covenant originally made with Abraham and giving Moses the Ten Commandments.

THE TEN COMMANDMENTS

1. You shall have no other Gods but me.
2. You shall not make idols or images in the form of God.
3. You shall not misuse the name of the Lord your God.
4. You shall remember and keep the Sabbath day holy.
5. Respect your father and your mother.
6. You shall not kill.
7. You shall not commit adultery.
8. You shall not steal.
9. You shall not give false evidence against your neighbor.
10. You shall not be envious of anything that belongs to your neighbor.

LATER HISTORY

As time passed, Judaism flourished in the region of Canaan, especially under such exalted kings as David (he who killed Goliath) and Solomon (he of the mines). It was the latter who built the first holy Jewish temple in Jerusalem. And yet the persecution of Jewish people continued. That first temple was destroyed by the Babylonians in 587 BC and the second temple was destroyed by the Romans in 70 CE. Over the following centuries, countless numbers of Jewish people were massacred, expelled from their homes or forced to convert to Christianity. The apex of their persecution came in the twentieth century, when six million Jewish people were systematically slaughtered across Nazi-occupied Europe.

Following the horrors of the Holocaust, many of the surviving Jewish people emigrated to the ancient homeland of their faith in the Middle East to embrace the notion of Zionism, a movement which sought the creation of a Jewish nation state there. This would become Israel, which became an officially recognized independent country in 1948. Today, though Jewish communities still exist around the world, most are based in Israel and the USA.

ASPECTS OF WORSHIP

The Synagogue

The Jewish house of worship is the synagogue. Aside from being the place where services are delivered, the synagogue is also crucial as a social gathering point for Jewish people and a place of sanctuary and community. Synagogues typically have their chairs or pews facing Jerusalem, and at the front is an ark containing a copy of the Torah scrolls, an eternal light (a lamp which is never extinguished to symbolize God's presence) above that ark, and a platform from which the Torah is read.

The Clergy

The clergy of Judaism is not hierarchical: all members of a congregation hold equal importance. Nevertheless, synagogues traditionally have a rabbi (a Torah scholar, who can be female in all but Orthodox Judaism), a cantor (who delivers the prayers) and sometimes a gabbai (who manages the other aspects of services) to lead each congregation.

The Dress

The traditional dress code for congregations encompasses two principal items. These are not mandatory, though many adherents choose to wear them, including outside the synagogue and in their everyday lives.

- Kippah—the skullcap worn by men (and sometimes women) to demonstrate their respect for God.
- Tallit—a prayer shawl worn during the prayer service.

THE SABBATH

The Sabbath (known in Hebrew as *Shabbat*) is Judaism's day of rest from work, commemorating the day when God rested after creating the universe (the word *Shabbat* literally means "he rested"). Beginning at sunset on Friday and lasting until sunset on Saturday, the Sabbath is a day of peace and holiness, normally celebrated with family. Food is especially important, and the three required meals (Friday night dinner, Saturday lunch and the final meal before sunset on Saturday) typically include traditional foods such as *challah* (braided bread), *gefilte fish* (stuffed fish), chicken soup, *cholent* (meat stew) and *kugel* (a pudding or casserole made from noodles or potato). Also typical are the synagogue services, such as the *Kabbalat Shabbat* (which means "receiving the Sabbath") on Friday evening to mark the beginning of the day of rest and the *Havdalah* (which means "separation") on Saturday at sunset to mark the end. It is customary to dress well not just for these services but for the whole day, and some choose to wear white on the Sabbath as a symbol of purity and holiness.

THE BAR MITZVAH / BAT MITZVAH

Bar mitzvah, meaning "son of the commandment," is both a designation and a celebration of what a boy becomes when he turns 13. The designation is that the boy becomes a bar mitzvah—in effect, a fully grown man, with all the moral and ethical responsibilities that entails. The celebration is often (but not always) held to mark this transition, involving the boy's first public recitation of a Torah passage, a speech about the Torah and a party. For girls, the bat mitzvah generally involves the same, though this happens at the age of 12 (or 13 in Reform Judaism).

MOSES

BORN: 1391 BC, Egypt

DIED: 1271 BC, modern-day Jordan (aged 120)

DIED OF: A "divine kiss" on top of Mount Nebo

WHERE WAS HE BURIED? Nobody knows. When Moses died, God buried him with no gravestone nor monument to mark the spot, ensuring that the Israelites would have nothing to worship as a false idol.

OCCUPATION: Leader / shepherd / Egyptian prince / prophet

OTHER NAMES: Moshe Rabbenu

DID HE HAVE A FAMILY? Exodus tells us that he married a priest's daughter called Zipporah and, with her, had two sons: Gershom and Eleazer.

THE WATER LEGENDS: Found as a baby in a river; parted the Red Sea.

DO NOT GIVE BACK TO HIS
MASTER A SERVANT WHO HAS
GONE IN FLIGHT FROM HIS
MASTER AND COME TO YOU:
LET HIM GO ON LIVING AMONG
YOU IN WHATEVER PLACE IS
MOST PLEASING TO HIM.

MOSES

Christianity

ORIGIN: First century CE, Judea (modern-day Israel/Palestine)

DEITY: God (Trinity of the Father, the Son and the Holy Spirit)

SYMBOL: Cross

KEY SCRIPTURE: Bible

MAJOR FIGURE: Jesus Christ

KEY FESTIVALS AND HOLY DAYS: Christmas Day, December 25th (celebration of the birth of Jesus); Easter, March/April (commemoration of the crucifixion and resurrection of Jesus)

NOTABLE BRANCHES: Roman Catholicism; Protestantism; Eastern Orthodoxy

ESTIMATED ADHERENTS: 2.1 billion (27.27 percent of world population)

Christianity is a religion of superlatives. The largest faith in the world, it has more adherents than any other and its churches can be found in most countries. Its key scripture, the Bible, is the best-selling book ever with over 5 billion copies sold, and the faith has been the state religion of some of the most powerful empires ever seen. Spawning more branches and denominations than many other religions combined, and with over two-thirds of all Americans declaring themselves as Christian, Christianity's success over the last two millennia from truly humble origins is nothing short of remarkable.

BELIEFS

Christianity is a religion which preaches the importance of love and forgiveness, though at its core it focuses on the spiritual and the divine, and the key beliefs of the faith can be summarized as follows:

1. There is only one God.
2. Jesus was the son of God, sent by his father to save humanity and redeem mankind's sins through this death.

3. God is a Trinity comprising the Father (God), the Son (Jesus, who was the human form of God) and the Holy Spirit (the continuing presence of God in mankind and the world).

4. There is an afterlife, with heaven reserved for those who accept Christ and hell for those who don't.

THE GOLDEN RULE IN CHRISTIANITY

"And as ye would that men should do to you, do ye also to them likewise."—Luke 6:31

EARLY HISTORY: THE STORY OF JESUS

The story begins in surroundings popularized by nativity scenes across the world: refused entry to a Bethlehem inn because there was no room, Mary of Nazareth, with her husband Joseph by her side, gave birth to Jesus in a stable, and the baby spent his first night in a manger surrounded by farm animals. Following a mysterious star which guided them to the stable, some magi (often known as "the three wise men") came to visit Jesus, bringing him gifts of gold, frankincense and myrrh (the latter two are types of incense), for they believed him to be the Messiah prophesied in the Torah (the Jewish Bible, known in Christianity as the Old Testament).

When word reached King Herod of Judea that a future King of the Jews had been born, he ordered the execution of all young Jewish boys. Since Jesus and his family were themselves Jewish, they fled to Egypt, returning to Nazareth only when it was safe to do so after Herod died around 4 BC. From there on, little is known about the early life of Jesus, except that it is likely he took his father's profession of carpenter. The story resumes when, at about the age of 30, he was baptized in the River Jordan by John the Baptist. After his baptism, Jesus spent 40 days in the desert, avoiding temptation by the Devil along the way, and returned to civilization to teach a gospel of faith, love and forgiveness.

His sermons—especially the Sermon on the Mount—began to attract attention, and when Jesus entered Jerusalem to crowds chanting "Hosanna!" (an Aramaic expression of praise and joy) at his arrival, the Jewish authorities grew concerned about the challenge he presented. Soon, betrayed by one of his disciples called Judas, Jesus was seized by the Jewish authorities and charged with blasphemy when he told them that he was the son of God. Handed over to the Romans, he was imprisoned, flogged and finally crucified: nailed to a cross and left to die. His dead body was placed in a tomb with a large stone sealing the entrance. However, when one of his followers, Mary Magdalene, came to anoint his body on the following Sunday, he had vanished. Resurrected, he appeared to Mary Magdalene and to the disciples a number of times before ascending to heaven, delivering on his final appearance the Great Commission: that his followers should go out into the world and make disciples wherever they went.

ASPECTS OF WORSHIP

The Church

Churches come in all shapes and sizes, from huge cathedrals to tiny chapels—indeed, a church can quite literally be anywhere, for a "church" can also simply mean a congregation of Christians. Common features include stained-glass windows, an altar and paintings of saints or biblical scenes, though none of these are prescribed or necessary. The one common feature shared by all churches is Christianity's symbol: the cross.

The Clergy

The clergy of Christianity is composed of ordained ministers who "lead" the religion, most commonly bishops, priests and deacons, although there are other orders, such as vicars, pastors and preachers, depending on the branch or denomination.

Christening

This is the ceremony where babies are formally given their names. Christenings often but not always include a baptism: the baby is doused in water to symbolize its admission into the Christian Church.

LATER HISTORY

Over the two centuries following the death of Jesus, the religion began to gain ground as churches were established and the writings that form the New Testament were compiled. And then, in the fourth century, the Roman Emperor Constantine converted to Christianity, giving the faith more clout and power and paving the way for it to be declared the official religion of the empire by Theodosius I in 380. Over time, Christianity spread, surviving the fall of the Roman Empire, surviving its own internal splits and schisms, and surviving the Crusades. It migrated to the New World and to Africa, where it continued to flourish without losing its stronghold in Europe. Today, Christianity is practiced on every single continent, with churches in places one might never expect—in a disused mine in southern Australia; in an oak tree in Seine-Maritime, France; on a bridge in Yorkshire; and even in Antarctica, where there are no fewer than eight.

THE THREE PRINCIPAL BRANCHES OF CHRISTIANITY

As Christianity has evolved over the two millennia since the birth of Christ, it has split and subdivided into a number of varying denominations. In the USA alone, there are over a thousand different branches. However, the three denominations which hold the greatest sway around the world are undoubtedly Roman Catholicism, Protestantism and Eastern Orthodoxy.

Eastern Orthodoxy

Five hundred years before the separation of Protestants and Catholics, an even greater split happened: the great East–West Schism. No longer recognizing the authority of the Western church based in Rome, the Eastern church based in Constantinople sought to remove itself from beneath the Catholic wing, and in 1054 the Western Pope Leo IX and the Eastern Patriarch Michael Cerularius simultaneously excommunicated each other. Eastern Orthodoxy became the official state religion of the

Byzantine Empire and, with approximately 270 million adherents today, it continues to dominate in Eastern Europe and the Caucasus.

Roman Catholicism

The godfather of all Christian denominations, Roman Catholicism was born in the fourth century when the Roman Empire adopted Christianity. With approximately 1.28 billion adherents today, Roman Catholicism is larger than both Protestantism and Eastern Orthodoxy combined. In the Catholic tradition, it was once the role of the apostles to maintain the Christian faith, and at the head of the apostles was St Peter, personally appointed by Jesus as the leader of the Church. Bishops became the successors to the apostles and, just as the former had Peter as their leader, the latter have the bishop of Rome—or, as he is more commonly known, the Pope. With his government of cardinals, the Pope is the supreme leader of the Catholic Church, and also the head of state of Vatican City, an independent city-state in Rome. It is here that the Pope lives in an enormous building called the Apostolic Palace, which features offices of the Catholic Church, residential rooms and apartments, private and public chapels, museums, libraries and the famous Sistine Chapel, with its ceiling painted by Michelangelo.

Protestantism

Protestantism, as its name suggests, began as a protest, kick-started in the sixteenth century by theologians such as Martin Luther and John Calvin, who condemned some of the doctrines and practices of the Roman Catholic Church. With approximately 920 million adherents today, Protestantism encompasses the highest number of different denominations and as such has no central governing body. Some of these denominations are discussed below.

Other Branches

AMISH

Amish people belong to a branch of Anabaptism, which is itself a branch of Protestantism. The roots of the Amish church can be found in Switzerland, though today most Amish live in the USA, especially in Pennsylvania. The group are famous (and often famously mocked) for their shunning of modern technology. Lifestyles are usually agrarian with horses and carts favored over cars, little to no use of electricity and plain, functional clothes. They are also known for their non-violent, hardworking and humble values. Another apparent difference is that, once a man is married, he is forbidden to shave his beard or grow a moustache.

QUAKERS

"Quaker" is the name given to a member of the Religious Society of Friends, a branch of Christianity dating back to the 1650s in England. In fact, the word "Quaker" started out as a term of derision used against the Friends (it was said that they would quake or physically shake during religious experiences), but they soon appropriated the word and used it for themselves, stripping it of negative connotations. However, the persecution from the Church of England continued and many Quakers emigrated. It was none other than a Quaker, William Penn, who moved to America and founded a colony called Pennsylvania where any religion could be practiced—the same Pennsylvania which is home to many Amish and Quaker families today.

Worship can be "programmed" or "unprogrammed:" programmed worship has readings, prayers and hymns; unprogrammed worship is when a group sits in silence until one of them feels inclined to speak—Quakers believe that this is God speaking through them.

MORMONS

There are various different Mormon churches (and approximately 16 million Mormons spread around the world), but the largest is the Church of Jesus Christ of Latter-day Saints. The key beliefs of this church are: baptism by immersion (when the baptized person is submerged completely underwater rather than simply having it sprinkled on them); the integral importance of family; and abstinence from alcohol, tobacco and caffeine. Many people think that polygamy (in which a man can be married to more than one woman) is regularly practiced in Mormonism—in fact, while some Mormon churches still adhere to this practice, the Church of Jesus Christ of Latter-day Saints has forbidden polygamy since 1890.

JESUS CHRIST

BORN: *c.*6–4 BC, Bethlehem

DIED: *c.*30 CE, Golgotha (aged 33—36)

DIED OF: Crucifixion

OCCUPATION: Teacher / Carpenter / Messiah

OTHER NAMES: Jesus of Nazareth ("Christ" was not Jesus' surname, but comes from the Greek "Christos" meaning "anointed one")

WHAT WAS HE LIKE AS A TEENAGER? One of the few accounts of Jesus' early life comes from the Gospel of Luke, which tells us that Mary and Joseph lost him in Jerusalem for three days. They finally found him in the temple courts talking with the masters, who were said to be astonished by the teenager's grasp of theology.

LOVE IS PATIENT, LOVE IS KIND. IT DOES NOT ENVY, IT DOES NOT BOAST, IT IS NOT PROUD. IT DOES NOT DISHONOR OTHERS, IT IS NOT SELF-SEEKING, IT IS NOT EASILY ANGERED, IT KEEPS NO RECORD OF WRONGS. LOVE DOES NOT DELIGHT IN EVIL, BUT REJOICES WITH THE TRUTH. IT ALWAYS PROTECTS, ALWAYS TRUSTS, ALWAYS HOPES, ALWAYS PERSEVERES. LOVE NEVER FAILS.

1 CORINTHIANS 13:4—8

Islam

ORIGIN: 622 CE, Arabian Peninsula

DEITY: Allah

SYMBOLS: The Star and Crescent; "Allah" in Arabic characters

KEY SCRIPTURE: Qur'an

MAJOR FIGURE: Muhammad

KEY FESTIVALS AND HOLY DAYS: Ramadan, in the ninth month of the lunar calendar (one month of daytime fasting); Eid al-Fitr, the end of Ramadan (the festival of fast-breaking)

NOTABLE BRANCHES: Sunni; Shi'a

ESTIMATED ADHERENTS: 1.5 billion (19.48 percent of world population)

The second largest religion in the world, and the youngest of the three great Abrahamic faiths, Islam comes from the Arabic word for "peace" and "submission." The same Arabic word is also the base for "Muslim," a follower of Islam, and "As-salamu alaikum," the traditional Muslim greeting, which means "Peace be upon you." Muslims believe that there is one god called Allah, and that peace can be found by submitting to him. Though its base is in the Middle East and North Africa, Islam has adherents all around the world, with countries as far away as Malaysia and the Maldives officially recognizing it as their state religion.

BELIEFS

Muslim life centers around the Five Pillars, a framework of religious duties which affirm an individual's faith in Islam.

1. *Shahadah*—meaning "to bear witness," *Shahadah* is the verbal profession of faith, and Muslims repeat it several times daily.
2. *Salat*—the act of prayer which takes place five times a day in the direction of Mecca.

3. *Zakat*—meaning "charity." Since they believe that everything they have ultimately comes from Allah, Muslims also believe that they should share what they have accumulated with others who are less fortunate.

4. *Sawm*—the process of fasting, which is observed throughout the month of Ramadan, but also at other times during the year depending upon individual inclinations. Fasting takes place during the day, and does not just include abstinence from food: liquids, smoking and sex are also prohibited.

5. *Hajj*—if they are physically and financially able, Muslims should make the *Hajj* (or pilgrimage) to Mecca at least once during their lifetime.

THE GOLDEN RULE IN ISLAM

"Nor can goodness and evil be equal. Repel [evil] with what is better: Then will he between whom and you was hatred become as it were your friend and intimate!"—Qur'an 41:34

EARLY HISTORY: THE PROPHET MUHAMMAD

In 570, Muhammad was born in Mecca on the Arabian Peninsula. As a young man, he worked as a merchant (first for his uncle, then for the woman who would later become his wife), traveling far and wide across the Middle East as part of a camel caravan. Even during these years, he was known as a deeply spiritual man, and would often make pilgrimages to sacred sites. It was during one of these that, while meditating in a cave on Mount Jabal al-Nour, the Angel Gabriel appeared to Muhammad and commanded him to repeat the sacred words of Allah. These words would go on to form the basis of the Qur'an. This was not the only time Muhammad was to receive such divine revelations, and by 613 he had begun to preach throughout Mecca his belief that there was only one god, and that all should devote their lives to him. Despite Muhammad's insistence that Allah was the only god, he acknowledged that he was not the first prophet, maintaining that Abraham, Moses and Jesus were prophets before him and should be respected as such.

Many of the Arabic tribes who lived in Mecca, or who visited it to carry out trade at the time, followed faiths inclined toward polytheism and idolatry. As Muhammad's teachings (which prohibited both the worship of idols and of any god other than Allah) began to spread, they considered him a threat. They forced Muhammad and his followers to emigrate to Medina in 622 (the first year of the Muslim calendar). From Medina the Muslim community grew substantially, eventually reaching such impressive numbers that they re-entered Mecca in 630 and converted most of the city's population to Islam. Under Muhammad's guidance over the next two years until his death, Islam gained momentum and prominence.

Following Muhammad's death, a caliphate (a system of leadership) was installed to continue the prophet's work and further the Muslim cause. The first caliph was Muhammad's father-in-law, Abu Bakr. This caliphate became immensely powerful and, under it, Arab Muslims conquered large swathes of the Middle East. As the centuries passed, more caliphates and Islamic dynasties grew, most notably the Ottoman Empire from the sixteenth to the twentieth century, whose rulers called themselves sultans but sometimes also caliphs, and under whose influence Islam was thrust into its dominant role across the Middle East.

SUNNI AND SHI'A

The two principal denominations of Islam are Sunni and Shi'a, with 85 percent of Muslims adhering to the former and 15 percent adhering to the latter. Both believe Allah to be the one true god, both believe in the prophecy of Muhammad, and both follow the teachings of the Qur'an. Nevertheless, there are some important differences between the two denominations—principally, their disagreement over who should have led the faith after Muhammad's death. The Sunnis believe that Muhammad intended for the next leader to be chosen by the Muslim community, and they chose Abu Bakr. However, the Shi'ites dispute this, believing that the correct line of succession was not a matter of community consensus but heritage, and that Muhammad's son-in-law Ali should have been the first caliph. Today, the few Islamic countries with Shi'a majorities are Iran, Iraq, Azerbaijan and Bahrain.

LATER HISTORY: THE OTTOMAN EMPIRE

Islam found footholds in Africa largely thanks to the Muslim merchants who traveled along the trade routes of the east coast and the Sahara. It pushed east into Asia via similar methods, though this was also helped by the Muslim armies who invaded parts of the Indian subcontinent. But it was the Ottoman Empire, established in 1299 by Sultan Osman I, which became the most powerful of all Islamic states, especially so when it conquered Constantinople from the crumbling Byzantine Empire in 1453, renamed it Istanbul and proclaimed it as the Ottoman capital. At its peak, the Ottoman Empire encompassed large parts of the Middle East, North Africa and Eastern Europe, and Islam thrived under it. It was the First World War which effectively disintegrated the Ottoman Empire, its territories divided among other countries. Yet, despite the fall of that empire, the strength of Islam has not abated. Indeed, it is currently the fastest-growing religion in the world, with some experts predicting it will overtake Christianity to become the world's largest religion by the end of the twenty-first century.

ASPECTS OF WORSHIP

The Mosque

Mosques (the English word for the Arabic *masjid*) are the Muslim places of worship and the centers of Islamic communities. Most feature a minaret (a thin tower with an open space at the top from which the call to prayer is made), a domed rooftop (to symbolize the vault of heaven), a prayer hall with prayer rugs, a *mihrab* (an ornamental niche that indicates the direction of Mecca) and an ablution area for *wudu* (ritual washing).

The Clergy

Islam has no official clergy, for the faith professes that each individual has a direct connection with Allah, and therefore intermediaries are unnecessary. Nevertheless, most Muslim communities choose a respected and knowledgeable member as their imam (the head of the community) to lead the services and prayers.

Dress

The basis of most traditional Muslim forms of dress is the notion of modesty. Muslims are encouraged not to draw attention to themselves as individuals. There are some requirements for male modesty (covering oneself from the navel to the knee, for example), but the rules tend to be stricter for women, with Muhammad himself instructing that women should cover all of their bodies except the face and hands. Many Muslim women wear a *hijab* (a scarf covering the head and neck but not the face), a *niqab* (a veil to cover the face, often worn in tandem with a *hijab*) or a *burka* (a garment which covers the whole body and has a grille for the face).

Mecca

Located in Saudi Arabia, Mecca is the birthplace of Muhammad and the holy city of Islam. Muslims pray toward it five times a day, and most make the *Hajj* (pilgrimage) to its *Kaaba*, the cube-shaped building in the center of the Great Mosque of Mecca. Non-Muslims are forbidden from entering Mecca.

HALAL OR HARAM?

Within the dietary laws of Islam, food can be divided into two categories: *halal* (meaning "permissible") and *haram* (meaning "forbidden"). The most basic distinction between the two is that, unless a type of food is specifically stated as haram in the Qur'an, it is halal. So what food does the Qur'an explicitly forbid? First and foremost, pork—pigs are considered as not just dirty animals, but impure and harmful to those who consume them. Most other animals can be eaten by Muslims, but they are only halal if they have been prepared according to Islamic law. For example, the slaughterer (a Muslim) must say "Bismillah" (meaning "in the name of God") before cutting the animal's throat with one motion—this is to ensure that the sacred life is taken quickly and painlessly and in the name of God. Drinks also fall into the categories of halal and haram, and any containing alcohol are absolutely forbidden: the Qur'an teaches that "intoxicants" are "abominations of Satan's handiwork" (5:90–91). Throughout the month of Ramadan, all food and drink becomes haram during daylight hours.

MUHAMMAD

BORN: 570, Mecca

DIED: 632, Medina (aged 62)

DIED OF: Unspecified illness

OCCUPATIONS: Merchant / Prophet

MARRIED: Muhammad had 13 wives, but considered to be the most important is Khadija, his first wife and first follower.

OTHER NAMES: The spelling "Muhammad" conforms to the strictest transliteration of the Arabic, though you may have seen his name spelled as "Mohammad," "Muhamed" or "Mahomet."

WHY ARE THERE NO IMAGES OF MUHAMMAD? Unlike the prophets and founders of other religions—many of whose depictions are ubiquitous—any kind of image (including pictures and statues) of Muhammad is forbidden in Islam, for it is believed that depictions encourage the worship of idols.

WHOEVER HOLDS FIRMLY TO
ALLAH HAS BEEN GUIDED
TO A STRAIGHT PATH.

QUR'AN 3:101

Hinduism

ORIGIN: *c.*2000 BC, India

DEITIES: 330 million, but Brahma, Vishnu and Shiva are generally recognized as the principal trinity

SYMBOL: Om (or Aum)

KEY SCRIPTURES: Bhagavad Gita; Vedas; Upanishads; Puranas

MAJOR FIGURE: Sri Krishna

KEY FESTIVALS AND HOLY DAYS: Diwali, five days in October/November (Festival of Lights); Holi, first day of spring (Festival of Colors)

NOTABLE BRANCHES: Vaishnavism, Shaivism, Shaktism and Smartism

ESTIMATED ADHERENTS: 1 billion (13 percent of world population)

Though most experts agree that Hinduism is the oldest surviving religion in the world, they can disagree profusely when it comes to actually defining it. Indeed, some even dispute whether it is a religion at all, preferring to label it a way of life (or, to use the Hindu term, a *dharma*). Its indefinable nature comes from the fact that there is no prescribed way to be a Hindu, with followers ranging from polytheistic to monotheistic and even to atheistic. Nevertheless, even if it isn't a religion but a way of life, it is a fundamentally *spiritual* way of life, encompassing beliefs and practices aimed at spiritual betterment. The *dharma* of Hinduism is a long-lasting and deeply venerated tradition, especially in India where it is the dominant faith: 80 percent of the country's population are Hindu.

BELIEFS

Specific beliefs within Hinduism can vary from area to area and even from person to person, but there are three core doctrines which form the basis of the Hindu tradition.

1.   *Samsara*—the cycle of rebirth

2. *Karma*—the law of cause and effect
3. *Moksha*—the notion of freedom

Both *samsara* and *karma* are universal and inevitable: we have always been and will always be reborn, and along the way we accrue positive or negative *karma* based upon our actions. Therefore, living a good and worthy life is not just beneficial to others but also to ourselves: goodness of both actions and thoughts will bring goodness to one's current and future lives. *Moksha* can mean several different forms of freedom depending on the particular school of thought. In some, it is freedom from negative states of mind, such as ignorance, anger or jealousy. In other schools, however, *moksha* can even mean freedom from *samsara* itself, and from the repeated suffering of endless rebirth.

THE GOLDEN RULE IN HINDUISM

"Those acts that you consider good when done to you, do those to others, none else."—Taittiriya Upanishad

HISTORY

Unlike the other religions of the Big Five, Hinduism has no specific human founder, and it is impossible to say precisely when the faith began. Many historians state that it probably coalesced as a synthesis of older spiritual beliefs and practices in the Indian subcontinent around 2000 BC, but it may have happened long before that. The word "Hindu" comes from the River Indus in northern India, and the earliest known use of the term comes from the sixth century BC, when Persians migrated to the area and called the river the "Hindu," the land "Hindustan" and its people "Hindus." What we do know is that the first written scriptures of Hinduism, the Vedas, were produced sometime around 1500 BC, and that it was the later Puranas—scriptures written between 500 BC and 1000 CE—which first recorded the stories of Hinduism's three principal deities: Brahma, Vishnu and Shiva.

THE GODS OF HINDUISM

With a pantheon of gods and goddesses unequalled by any of the other major world religions, Hinduism is peppered with a colorful array of deities. The supreme being Brahman (not to be confused with the god Brahma) is the spiritual core of the universe, and in some schools of Hindu thought all the other deities are simply different forms of Brahman—among them the many-armed elephant Ganesha (god of success); the monkey-faced Hanuman (god of strength); the beautiful Lakshmi (goddess of wealth) and the formidable Kali (goddess of death). Perhaps the most important, however, is the trinity of Brahma, Vishnu and Shiva.

Brahma the Creator

The god Brahma (who is often considered to be the son of the supreme being Brahman, and has four heads, four arms and red skin) created the universe and all life within it and presides over it for a single day—the equivalent of four billion years. At the end of this day, Brahma will die and the universe will dissolve.

Vishnu the Preserver

Immaculately peaceful, Vishnu sustains life in the universe and is the upholder of all that is righteous and true. In order to maintain these principles, he has come to earth in a number of different incarnations— that of a tortoise called Kurma, a fish called Matsya, and in various human forms: most notably as Sri Krishna (see p.69).

Shiva the Destroyer

With a serpent coiled around his neck and the River Ganges cascading from his hair, Shiva is responsible for the death and destruction present in the universe. But there is no malice in his actions. Instead, Shiva destroys so that creation—and rebirth—may continue from what has died.

REINCARNATION

Another word for *samsara* (the cycle of rebirth which forms a key tenet of Hindu belief) is the more widely recognized "reincarnation." Unlike the Abrahamic notions of heaven and hell, Hinduism's afterlife is one in which the soul keeps getting reborn as a new life and in a new body over and over again.

Some aspects of reincarnation are beyond our control: we cannot take any physical things we have accrued in this life (such as money or possessions) into the next, nor can we take our memories or wisdom. However, some Hindus believe that they do have control over some things—for example, that they can move up or down the caste system (a form of hierarchy within their society) in their next life depending on their actions in their current life. This is *karma*, and it's almost the epitome of the Golden Rule. If your actions are good, you will receive positive karma. If your actions are evil, you will receive negative karma. The more positive karma you accrue in your lifetime, the more likely it is that you will be reborn in a life similar to or better than your current; the more negative karma you accrue in your lifetime, the more likely it is that you will be reborn in a life worse than your current. And this may not even be as a human, for all life is subject to *samsara*. According to Hinduism, it is possible that one day in the future you will be reborn as a wasp, and that in the past you have already been a wasp.

If this all sounds too much to bear, then thankfully there is *moksha*, the escape route from the cycle of rebirth. Many Hindus believe that salvation from *samsara* is possible once a soul has abandoned all desires and goals (paradoxically, you need to abandon the goal of *moksha* in order to attain it) and accepted that it is itself one and the same soul as the supreme being, Brahman.

ASPECTS OF WORSHIP
The Temple
Temples (or *mandirs*) are the Hindu places of *puja* (worship). They usually contain a central shrine featuring *murtis* (sacred images) and *yantras* (diagrams of the universe) where priests recite the Vedas to assembled worshippers.

The Pilgrimage

Pilgrimages are highly important in Hinduism, and sacred sites include temples, rivers and mountains, mostly in India. One of the most important places for Hindus, often touted as the religious capital of India, is the city of Varanasi, which is dedicated to Shiva. Pilgrims come from far and wide to visit the numerous *ghats* (riverfront steps) and to bathe in the river at sunrise, washing away their sins and sufferings in the process.

SRI KRISHNA

BORN: *c.*3228 BC, Mathura, India

DIED: *c.*3102 BC, northern India (age 125)

DIED OF: An arrow to the ankle (a hunter mistook him for a deer)

HE MUST HAVE BEEN FURIOUS: On the contrary, in his final words he blessed the hunter.

OCCUPATIONS: Teacher / Yogi / Charioteer / Messenger

HUMAN OR GOD? Sri Krishna is considered to be a human incarnation of the god Vishnu.

DID HE PRESERVE LIFE LIKE VISHNU? Yes, with his kindness and his actions, but he took life too. When a sage told his uncle Kamsa that he (Kamsa) would be killed by one of his own nephews, Kamsa set about having each of his nephews murdered. Sri Krishna's parents managed to get Sri Krishna to safety, and yet Kamsa persisted, relentlessly sending assassins to kill Sri Krishna. When he was old enough, Sri Krishna took his safety into his own hands and fulfilled the prophecy by killing his uncle.

SET THY HEART UPON THY WORK, BUT NEVER ON ITS REWARD.

BHAGAVAD GITA

Buddhism

ORIGIN: Fifth century BC, India

DEITY: None

SYMBOLS: Dharma wheel; Lotus flower

KEY SCRIPTURES: Tipitaka; Prajnaparamita Sutras; Kanjur

MAJOR FIGURES: Siddhartha Gautama (the Buddha); the Dalai Lama

KEY FESTIVALS AND HOLY DAYS: Vesak, on a full moon day in May (the Buddha's birthday); Asalha Puja, on the first full moon of the eighth lunar month, usually in July (commemoration of the Buddha's first teaching)

NOTABLE BRANCHES: Theravada; Mahayana; Tibetan Buddhism

ESTIMATED ADHERENTS: 350 million (4.55 percent of world population)

Buddhism is often thought of as the epitome of a peaceful religion, with its focus on meditation, compassion and release from suffering. It grew out of Hinduism (and can be seen as a reaction to the inevitabilities of rebirth and suffering which that religion professes) in the fifth century BC in India from the teachings of the Buddha: Siddhartha Gautama (see p.82). It is still predominantly an Eastern religion, and most Buddhists today live in China, with Thailand home to the second-largest number and Japan home to the third.

BELIEFS

The Four Noble Truths as taught by Siddhartha Gautama in his inaugural sermon (and repeatedly thereafter) form the first cornerstone of Buddhist belief.

1. *Dukkha*—there is suffering in life.
2. *Samudaya*—suffering is caused by desire and attachment.
3. *Nirhodha*—suffering can be ended by ending desire and attachment.

4. *Magga*—freedom from suffering can be found by following a specific path.

In essence, the Four Noble Truths tell us that, though suffering exists in life, it can be ended if we follow the right path. This path, the second cornerstone of Buddhism, is known as the Eightfold Path, or as the Middle Way of moderation and how to live "right." By following the Eightfold Path, Buddhists can break the cycle of rebirth and suffering and achieve enlightenment:

1. Right understanding
2. Right thought
3. Right speech
4. Right action
5. Right livelihood
6. Right effort
7. Right mindfulness
8. Right concentration

THE GOLDEN RULE IN BUDDHISM

"Hurt not others in ways that you yourself would find hurtful."—Udanavarga

EARLY HISTORY: THE STORY OF THE BUDDHA

Sometime around 560 BC in the Indian subcontinent, the Buddha was born as Prince Siddhartha Gautama. Wealthy and sheltered from the hardships of the world as he was, it was not until he grew into a young adult that he left his palace-home in disguise and witnessed the pain and suffering of ordinary people. The experience changed him forever. He became devoted to finding a deeper meaning to life than the one he had thus far enjoyed. So, renouncing his lifestyle (and his wife and son with it), he moved to the forests to experience a more ascetic life. This period of extreme poverty and fasting, however, still left him feeling unfulfilled, and so he came up with the Middle Way of moderation, finding a path between the extremes of luxury and deprivation. Six years later, under the shade of a Bodhi tree, he meditated in pursuit of nirvana (the release from rebirth, like the Hindu *moksha*) and enlightenment. After surviving many tests to his resilience, Gautama finally found what he sought, remaining in the blissful consciousness of nirvana for many days and achieving enlightenment.

On his return to the physical world, the Buddha (which means "the enlightened one") resolved to teach others what he had learned, traveling across much of the Indian subcontinent to deliver sermons to whomever would listen. His sermons attracted attention and gained followers largely because they focused on the practicalities of how to escape suffering and rebirth and achieve enlightenment, rather than talking about deities and how to impress them. Within these sermons, he established the Four Noble Truths and the Eightfold Path, along with his avowals of the importance of love, compassion and generosity.

ASPECTS OF WORSHIP
The Temples
In China and Japan, Buddhist temples usually take the form of a pagoda, with multiple levels, a spire and a Chinese-style roof. Across the rest of the Buddhist world, most other temples are stupas, a bell-shaped structure. Buddhist monks and nuns live in monasteries, which can be connected to temples

but are not always. Nevertheless, monasteries are also considered sacred places of worship.

The Prayers
If Buddhists don't believe in a god, why do they pray? There are a number of different answers: many Buddhists believe that, while he is not a god in the western sense of the word, the Buddha is an enlightened being who can be prayed to; others believe that what they chant to the Buddha is not so much a prayer as a vow or offering; and, of course, some denominations of Buddhism (such as Tibetan Buddhism) do indeed feature deities.

Buddhist prayers, or mantras, can also be delivered in a variety of ways. You can say them, or you can have them written onto prayer flags or prayer wheels. Every time you spin a prayer wheel or the wind blows your prayer flag, the mantras are released out into the world. The most well-known Buddhist prayer is *Om mani padme hum*—a difficult mantra to interpret, but one generally translated as "Praise to the jewel in the lotus:" a prayer directed toward one of Buddhism's sacred symbols, the lotus flower, or perhaps more specifically toward a bodhisattva (a being on the path to Buddhahood) called Avalokiteśvara.

LATER HISTORY

After the Buddha's death, his followers began to organize Buddhism as a religious movement, and the faith quickly gained ground, even becoming the state religion of India under Ashoka the Great in the third century BC. From there, it spread throughout the East, subdividing along the way into three primary branches: Theravada, Mahayana and Tibetan Buddhism. Though it never succeeded in achieving the predominance of Hinduism in India, of Islam in the Middle East and of Christianity in the western world, Buddhism continues to be practiced across the world, particularly in South East Asia.

THE THREE PRIMARY BRANCHES

Theravada—the oldest of the three, Theravada is considered to be the most conservative Buddhist denomination. Its language is Pali (the language of Siddhartha Gautama), and it places emphasis on silent, mindful meditation and the application of personal insight and knowledge to reach nirvana. Today, it is practiced mostly in South East Asia.

Mahayana—Mahayana takes a more social approach to Buddhism. With Sanskrit as its language, mantras and chanting (often performed in groups) are given greater emphasis than silent meditation, and its adherents believe that the enlightenment of all rather than just oneself should be sought. Though it is approximately 400 years younger than Theravada, Mahayana is currently the largest Buddhist tradition, practiced mostly in the north-eastern part of Asia.

Tibetan Buddhism—as its name suggests, this is the principal form of Buddhism in Tibet, though it is also widely practiced across other Himalayan regions (such as Bhutan). A melding of Mahayana Buddhism and the ancient religion of the Tibetan people, Bon, it is one of the most complex and intricate forms of Buddhism, filled with the gods and deities of Bon. Also unlike Theravada and Mahayana, Tibetan Buddhism has a leader of the tradition: the Dalai Lama.

THE DALAI LAMA

The concept of "Dalai-Lamaism" depends upon reincarnation. Each Dalai Lama is a reincarnation of his predecessor, and therefore a reincarnation of all of them as the same spirit passes from body to body through the ages. He is ultimately the living incarnation of Avalokiteśvara (*Chenresig* in Tibetan), revered in Tibetan Buddhism as the same bodhisattva of compassion prayed to in the *Om mani padme hum* mantra, and the patron of Tibet. The name "Dalai Lama" comes from a Mongol phrase meaning "Ocean of Wisdom," which the Mongol king Altan Khan bestowed upon the first recognized Dalai Lama in the late sixteenth century. The current Dalai Lama, Tenzin Gyatso, is the fourteenth—born in 1935 in a then independent Tibet, enthroned at the age of 16, and then forced to flee to India when China annexed Tibet in 1959. He has not returned since, and currently lives in Dharamsala in India, the seat of the Tibet-in-exile government. Traditionally, the Dalai Lama has held absolute power over spiritual and political matters in the Tibetan theocracy, but the current Dalai Lama has worked tirelessly to transform his government into a democracy. In 1990, the Tibet-in-exile government's new Dharamsala cabinet was elected not by the Dalai Lama, but by—for the first time in Tibet's history—a democratic process. Although Tenzin Gyatso retired from the role of Tibet's political leader in 2011, many Tibetans still revere him as such, for the absolute authority of the Dalai Lama is an unquestionable part of their faith.

SIDDHARTHA GAUTAMA

BORN: *c.*560 BC, Lumbini (in modern-day Nepal)

DIED: *c.*460 BC, Kushinagar, northern India (exact age unknown)

DIED OF: Natural causes

OCCUPATIONS: Teacher / Prince / Buddha

OTHER NAMES: The Buddha / The Enlightened One / Gotama / Sakyamuni

THE BUDDHA'S BIG BELLY: Many pictures and statues of the Buddha depict him as rather fat, although this is extremely unlikely. In accordance with following the Middle Way of moderation, Gautama would have avoided both feasting and fasting, and would therefore have probably been of average build. It is believed that this "laughing buddha" image is actually of a Chinese monk (possibly called Budai).

IF WITH A PURE MIND A
PERSON SPEAKS OR ACTS,
HAPPINESS FOLLOWS
THEM LIKE A NEVER-
DEPARTING SHADOW.

BUDDHA

OTHER MAJOR
RELIGIONS

The Big Five may dominate the majority of religious thoughts and practices across the world, but there are also myriad other faiths out there which, though they may not be as widely known, are of no less importance. Indeed, their histories, prophets and practices are just as fascinating as those we discovered among the Big Five. In this chapter, you'll find out why Sikhs wear turbans, what exactly Confucius said, which religion gave us acupuncture, and how to correctly enter a Shinto shrine. Largely distributed among Asian and Middle Eastern countries, and with over 60 million adherents between them, the following major religions have a profound influence.

Sikhism

ORIGIN: *c.*1500, Punjab region of India

DEITY: God (one interchangeable name used to denote God is Akal Purakh)

SYMBOL: The Khanda

KEY SCRIPTURE: Guru Granth Sahib

MAJOR FIGURE: Guru Nanak

KEY FESTIVALS AND HOLY DAYS: Vaisakhi, April 13th or 14th (celebrates the founding of the Khalsa, a group of warrior-saints); Bandi Chhor Divas, on the same five days as Hinduism's Diwali in October/November (renowned for its illumination of Sikh temples)

ESTIMATED ADHERENTS: Approx. 27 million (0.35 percent of world population)

One of the youngest world religions, Sikhism emerged in that birthplace of so many other faiths: pre-colonial India. While it incorporated many of the themes of the country's two dominant religions—Hinduism and Islam—it also sought to differentiate itself from them in important areas, chiefly that of equality. Guru Nanak, the founder of Sikhism, denounced the idea of a caste system, although such a system can still be found within Sikh communities.

BELIEFS

Perhaps the most succinct way to summarize the core beliefs of Sikhism is to look at the three duties Sikhs must adhere to:

1. *Nam japna*—Godliness. God should always be in one's thoughts.
2. *Kirt karna*—Work. To work earnestly and honestly, whether for a livelihood or within one's own home.
3. *Vand chhakna*—Sharing. Both in and beyond one's community.

At the core of Sikhism is one God, who has neither form nor gender, and who is worshipped in temples called *gurdwara* (literally, the "Doorway to God"). Yet, while godliness is central, the well-being of humans is also a hugely important part of the faith. Both *kirt karna* and *vand chhakna* demonstrate this importance: all humans are equal before God, and all should strive to recognize this through kind and harmonious living.

EARLY HISTORY: THE FIRST OF THE TEN GURUS

Sikhism evolved through the teachings of the Ten Gurus between the sixteenth and eighteenth centuries. The first of these was Guru Nanak, who was born into a Hindu family in 1469. Though he studied both Hinduism and Islam, he rejected many of their tenets, refusing—even at the age of 11—to wear a *janeo*: the length of thread worn over the shoulder by men to show their high caste. At the age of 30, he disappeared for three days, returning with the proclamation that he would no longer follow Hinduism or Islam, but instead would simply follow God's path. After this, he traveled far and wide to teach his philosophy. Just one day before he died, he appointed one of his followers the Second Guru.

LATER HISTORY: THE ELEVENTH OF THE TEN GURUS

Following Guru Nanak's example, before each succeeding Guru passed away, he mentored and then nominated the next, who would continue to lead and refine the religion. This tradition continued until the Tenth Guru, Gobind Singh, appointed the Eleventh Guru in the early eighteenth century to maintain the Guruship eternally, because he appointed the Guru Granth Sahib, the key scripture of the Sikh faith.

THE FIVE Ks

During the Tenth Guru's tenure, he instigated a dress code: the "Five Ks" which Sikhs should wear.

- *Kesh*—uncut hair to show respect for the perfection of God's creation (covered by a turban).
- *Kangha*—a small wooden comb to signify cleanliness.
- *Kara*—a circular bangle to symbolize the eternity of God.
- *Kachera*—underwear fastened by a drawstring, which marks the control of sexual desire.

Kirpan—a dagger for self-defense and, more importantly, the protection of others.

GURU NANAK

BORN: 1469, Nankana, Punjab (in modern-day Pakistan)

DIED: 1539, Kartarpur, Punjab (aged 69)

DIED OF: Natural causes

OCCUPATION: Guru (Teacher)

MARRIED: Mata Sulakkhani

THE LEGEND OF THE FLOWERS: When Guru Nanak died, his Hindu and Muslim followers argued over which funeral rites to choose for him. However, when the cloth covering his body was opened, it was said that it revealed nothing but hundreds of flowers, allowing Hindus and Muslims alike to take a flower each and remember his passing in harmony.

FROM ITS BRILLIANCY EVERYTHING IS ILLUMINATED.

GURU NANAK

Zoroastrianism

ORIGIN: *c.*600 BC, Persia (present-day Iran)

DEITY: Ahura Mazda

SYMBOLS: Faravahar; The sacred fire

KEY SCRIPTURES: Avesta

MAJOR FIGURE: Zoroaster

KEY FESTIVALS: Frawardigan, a ten-day festival over the New Year period around March 21st (to commemorate the souls of the dead); Sadeh, a bonfire festival which takes place around January 30th (100 days after the first day of winter)

ESTIMATED ADHERENTS: Approx. 190,000 (0.002 percent of world population)

One of the earliest monotheistic religions (pre-dating Christianity by at least six centuries, and possibly more—no one can be certain), Zoroastrianism centers around the motto: "Good thoughts, good words, good deeds." Founded by the prophet Zoroaster, it reached spectacular heights as the state religion of the mighty Persian Empire, remaining so for over a thousand years.

BELIEFS

1. *Humata* (Good thoughts)
2. *Hukhta* (Good words)
3. *Huveshta* (Good deeds)

Or, in a nutshell, goodness. Live a good life, Zoroastrianism teaches, and you will be rewarded beyond death. Live a wicked life, and you will be punished. Embodying these notions of goodness and wickedness are two perpetually warring spirits: Spenta Mainyu (the good) and Angra Mainyu (the wicked). However, humans are no passive observers in the battle between these spirits. Living a good life will not only help the individual, it will also help Spenta Mainyu and, thus, help save the world from evil.

HISTORY

Few religions have experienced a rise and fall of popularity quite as dizzying as Zoroastrianism's. From its humble and controversial beginnings as the prophet Zoroaster's radical rejection of polytheistic beliefs in his native Indo-Iranian homeland, it was adopted by the Persian Empire around 600 BC, thereby becoming one of the most powerful religions in the world. And, though it held this position for over a millennium, it was replaced in the seventh century CE by the rise of Islam, as many Zoroastrians converted to the new religion. Today, fewer than 200,000 Zoroastrians remain around the world; only 25,000 of them still live in Iran. Nevertheless, Zoroastrianism retains a remarkable level of importance, since it effectively set the groundwork for lots of other faiths in terms of religious concepts. It's where the original idea of heaven and hell came from, as well as the notions of a Messiah and being judged after death.

FIRE

Alongside the Faravahar, one of the most important symbols in Zoroastrianism is fire. Fire represents both the eternal power of the deity Ahura Mazda and the importance of purification. That's why, if you enter a Zoroastrian temple, you will see a fire burning. These are kept lit at all times, and many have been burning for years (or, in some cases, perhaps centuries). The priests who maintain them (with offerings of wood) wear masks so that their breath does not desecrate the sanctity of these fires.

THE PARSI

As Islam overtook Zoroastrianism as the dominant religion in the seventh century, a community known as the Parsi migrated to Gujarat in India to escape persecution. One quite beautiful Parsi folktale tells of their arrival: their ships were met by the local king, who presented them with a glass of milk filled to the brim to suggest that there was no room for them. The Parsi responded by adding some sugar to the milk to symbolize that, should they be allowed to stay, they would blend into and even sweeten their environment. Whether this story is true or not, the Parsi were indeed given refuge in Gujarat, and have succeeded in melding the region's customs (most Parsi today speak Gujarati as a first language) with their own, thereby keeping the fire of Zoroastrianism alive today.

ZOROASTER

BORN: Disputed, but possibly 628 BC, Rhages (in modern-day Iran)

DIED: Disputed, but possibly 551 BC (exact age unknown)

DIED OF: Assassinated during prayer by the priest of a rival cult

OCCUPATION: Prophet / Priest

LANGUAGE SPOKEN: Avestan (from which the Avesta takes its name)

OTHER NAMES: Zarathustra

ALSO A PROPHET IN: Islam, Baha'i, Manichaeism

BORN OF HUMANS OR ANGELS? According to legend,

both. It is said that his father, a priest, had an angel trapped inside him (the angel had entered a plant which Zoroaster's father consumed), and that his mother had the glory of heaven trapped inside her (it having entered her bosom as a ray of light). When the father and mother consummated their marriage, the angel and the divine ray of light conceived Zoroaster.

"Doing good to others is not a duty. It is a joy, for it increases your own health and happiness."

ZOROASTER

Confucianism

ORIGIN: *c.*500 BC, China

DEITY: None

SYMBOLS: The Chinese characters for "Confucius," "water," "scholar" and the Yin-Yang

KEY SCRIPTURES: The Four Books (The Analects of Confucius; The Great Learning; The Book of Mencius; The Doctrine of the Mean)

MAJOR FIGURE: Confucius

KEY FESTIVALS AND HOLY DAYS: Birthday of Confucius, September 28th (which kicks off a ten-day festival); Tomb Sweeping Day, April 4th or 5th (when ancestors are revered and their graves swept)

ESTIMATED ADHERENTS: Approx. 6 million (0.09 percent of world population)

Created by the eponymous Confucius in the sixth century BC, Confucianism became China's official state religion in the second century BC, and remained so for over 2,000 years. That it was able to retain its hold for so long over one of the largest countries in the world (almost 40 times the size of the UK) with one of the most diverse populations (over 50 different ethnic groups) is a testament to the intuitive and down-to-earth nature of this religion.

BELIEFS

Confucianism is based on five virtues which adherents should practise at all times:

1. Honesty
2. Benevolence
3. Knowledge
4. Politeness
5. Integrity

The fundamental principle in all five is respect: respect for yourself, respect for others and respect for humanity in general. Sound familiar? It's the famous Golden Rule—treat others as you want to be treated—which we've seen in each of the Big Five religions. Confucianism is one of the oldest known proponents of the Golden Rule.

EARLY HISTORY

During Confucius' life, China was in the midst of a period of social upheaval. Confucius hoped to address this by encouraging everyone (rulers included) to become kinder toward each other and more virtuous. Unfortunately, this conflicted with the idea that the emperor's power was divine (and that he could be as cruel as he liked), so it was not well received. It took 400 years, the changing of dynasties and the burning of a lot of Confucian books before an emperor would implement Confucianism as the official religion of China.

LATER HISTORY

After more than two millennia, the undoing of Confucianism came in the twentieth century as China shifted from empire to republic, finally losing most of its adherents during Chairman Mao's attempts to purge China of the religion (he considered Confucius a "class enemy"). Nevertheless, although Confucianism as a religion never really spread beyond the borders of China, the general ideas of Confucius himself have enjoyed popularity around the world, and continue to do so to this day.

PHILOSOPHY OR RELIGION?

Debates have raged for centuries over the correct definition of Confucianism. Is it a religion, or is it more a philosophy? It has no gods to speak of, no churches and no priests. But are these things necessary to make a religion a religion? Most sects of Buddhism are free of gods, many Christians believe a church can be anywhere so long as it has a congregation, and, with all the unspeakable things that have happened to priests (or been done by them) over the years, perhaps it's a kindness to be rid of them. To bridge the gap between the two sides of the debate and (in a beautifully Confucian way) find some harmony, many choose to refer to Confucianism simply as a belief system.

CONFUCIUS

BORN: 551 BC, China

DIED: 479 BC, China (aged 72)

DIED OF: Natural causes

OCCUPATION: Teacher / philosopher / scholar

BIRTH NAME: Kong Qiu

SO WHY DO WE CALL HIM CONFUCIUS? As a teacher, he was known as Kong Fuzi (Mandarin for "Master Kong"), which, thanks to the remarkably poor pronunciation of visiting Jesuits, became "Confucius" in the western world.

DOES HE HAVE ANY DESCENDANTS THAT WE KNOW OF? The answer is yes. About two million of them.

CONFUCIUS HE SAY… WHAT, EXACTLY? Quite a lot, as it happens. Anyone who has ever heard the grammatically (and ethically) dubious "Confucius he say…" will be aware that the man is one of the most quoted in history.

EVERYTHING HAS BEAUTY, BUT NOT EVERYONE SEES IT.

CONFUCIUS

Daoism

ORIGIN: *c.*500 BC, China

DEITIES: A multitude, but The Three Pure Ones are considered the most important

SYMBOLS: Dao, Yin-Yang

KEY SCRIPTURES: Dao De Jing; I Ching

MAJOR FIGURE: Laozi

KEY FESTIVAL: Hungry Ghost Festival, the fourteenth day of the seventh lunar month (a celebration during the Hungry Ghost Month, when the gates of hell are open and starving ghosts come to visit the living)

ESTIMATED ADHERENTS: Approx. 12 million (0.18 percent of world population)

You might know this religion as "Taoism," but the transliteration of Chinese has changed over recent years (*Peking* became *Beijing*; *Mao Tse-tung* became *Mao Zedong*, etc.) and "Daoism" has become the most commonly accepted spelling. But, while the letters may have changed, the religion itself has remained marvellously unaltered for almost two and a half millennia. "Dao" literally means "The Way:" a particular rhythm of the universe with which we can live in harmony if we follow certain steps.

BELIEFS

The principal virtues of Daoism are known as the Three Treasures, or *sanbao*:

1. Compassion
2. Frugality
3. Humility

Aside from these Three Treasures, at the very core of Daoism is the concept of *wu wei*. In much the same way as Buddhism teaches us to cast aside the individual ego, *wu wei* encapsulates the art of letting go. However, whereas in Buddhism the aim is to achieve enlightenment, in Daoism *wu wei* is a way to live perfectly in the natural world—to adopt both effortless calmness and spontaneous awareness, so that one's life becomes aligned with the unity of the universe. Some call this the "action of non-action."

HISTORY

While the fundamental principles of Daoism are fairly straightforward, its history is far from it. Dates and places and even reasons for its emergence remain heavily disputed. Did it begin with Laozi and his book *Dao De Jing* in the sixth century BC? Or did it originate even earlier, as a prehistoric folk religion in rural parts of China? What we do know is that, despite competition from Buddhism and Confucianism (whose founders were possibly contemporaries of Laozi), Daoism's popularity flourished from the third century BC onward, eventually becoming China's official state religion under the Tang Dynasty in the early eighth century. But it didn't last. Daoism slowly fell from favor under later dynasties such as the Yuan (who burned many Daoist texts in the thirteenth century) and the Qing (who rejected Daoism in favor of Confucianism). And then, of course, came Chairman Mao and his Cultural Revolution, when a large number of

Daoist temples were destroyed. Since the 1980s, however, there has been a resurgence in Daoism's popularity across China: temples have been restored, books reprinted, and there are currently around 25,000 Daoist monks and nuns practicing and perpetuating the tradition.

PRACTICES

We have Daoism to thank for a number of well-known practices around the world, including the following two:

Acupuncture—the technique of inserting a multitude of tiny needles into specific parts of the body. Daoists believe that the energy which creates and then sustains life is the "qi." Acupuncture is a method of treating, regulating, restoring or maintaining the body's "qi."

Qigong—another way of cultivating one's "qi," this time through prescribed movement. Somewhere between yoga and t'ai chi, qigong enhances physical health, improving, among other things, balance and flexibility. Yet it is also said to improve the spiritual aspect of the body, aiding the simultaneous letting go and awareness that *wu wei* propounds.

I CHING

The *I Ching* is a philosophical text offering guidance for the present and future. Though it pre-dates Daoism by at least 500 years, Daoism incorporated the text and its precepts into the heart of the Daoist tradition. To use the *I Ching*, start by thinking of a question you want answered. Then, toss three coins a total of six times. A numerical value will be assigned to each pattern the coins fall into after being tossed. These numerical values correspond to specific types of lines in the *I Ching*—the six lines you create will form a hexagram. There are 64 possible variations of these hexagrams. By consulting the *I Ching*, you can find the meaning of the hexagram you have created and use it to interpret an answer to your question.

LAOZI

BORN: *c.* Fifth century BC, Changzhou, China

DIED: *c.* Fifth century BC, Changzhou, China (age unknown)

DIED OF: Unknown

OCCUPATION: Philosopher / scholar

BIRTH NAME: Li Er

OTHER NAMES: Lao Tzu / Supremely Mysterious and Primordial Emperor

BUT DID HE EXIST? Though Laozi is one of the most revered figures in Chinese history, many people believe that he never even existed. The fact that his name literally means "old master" has led many to state that he was more of a Platonic ideal than a genuine living being, an amalgamation of all the original teachers and scribes of Daoism. Laozi's "history" is rife with conflicting yet nonetheless glorious stories—that he lived to be 990 years old, that he traveled to India to teach the Buddha, that he traveled to India and *became* the Buddha, and even that he was born as a greying and bearded 80-year-old man.

"A journey of a thousand miles must begin with a single step."

LAOZI

Shinto

ORIGIN: *c.*500 CE, Japan

DEITIES: Many, though Izanagi and Izanami are the central duo

SYMBOL: Torii (a traditional Japanese gate)

KEY SCRIPTURES: Kojiki; Shiko Nihongi

MAJOR FIGURE: Hirata Atsutane (1776–1843), a scholar and theologian

KEY FESTIVALS: Seijin Shiki, January 15th (when men and women aged 20 celebrate reaching adulthood); Shichigosan, the Sunday nearest November 15th (when parents take their children to shrines to thank the gods for their childhood)

ESTIMATED ADHERENTS: Approx. 4 million (0.05 percent of world population)

Taken from the Japanese characters *shin*, meaning the spirits or gods, and *to*, meaning the path or way (much like Daoism's *dao*), Shinto is literally the Way of the Gods.

Note the plural in the last word. Shinto has numerous gods, many of which stem from the animist spirits worshipped in Japanese folklore. Although Japan has outstripped most other countries around the world in its pursuit of modernity, the ancient rituals and practices of Shinto remain deeply entrenched in its traditions.

BELIEFS

The linchpins of Shinto are its Four Affirmations:

1. Family and tradition
2. Love of nature
3. Physical cleanliness
4. Worship of the gods (the *shin* or *kami*)

Overall, Shinto is about harmony: harmony with one's family, harmony with nature, harmony with the gods. Physical cleanliness is a way of assisting this harmony, but so too is mental cleanliness—for example, sincerity is deeply important in Shinto, and much of Japanese etiquette rests on this principle. However, there are no

moral absolutes, and how can there be when the gods—
the *kami*—themselves are imperfect beings and entirely
capable of committing wrongdoing?

HISTORY

Before Shinto, both Confucianism and Buddhism were
introduced to Japan through China, with Buddhism
going on to became Japan's state religion in the sixth
century. The emergence of Shinto can be seen as a
kind of nationalistic response to these Chinese imports.
Written in the eighth century, the Kojiki (one of Shinto's
principal texts) drew heavily from Japan's ancient beliefs
of worshipping nature-spirits and ancestors, providing the
people of Japan with a religion that was distinctly Japanese,
as opposed to the Chinese leanings of Buddhism and
Confucianism. However, it was not until the eighteenth
century that Buddhism was formally overthrown and
Shinto was instated as the official state religion, remaining
as such until Japan's defeat in the Second World War,
when the American General Douglas MacArthur ordered
the separation of faith and state.

KAMI

Gods. Spirits. *Shin*. *Kami*. No matter what you call them, they are everywhere in Shinto. Not just in entities such as mountains or streams, but in processes too. Rain has its *kami*. So does fertility. In fact, even people, after they die, have their own *kami* who lives on in spirit form. As a result, listing each would require a book far, far longer than this one. But among the key *kami* depicted in the narrative of the Kojiki are:

- **Izanagi** and **Izanami**—respectively, the male and female gods who came together to create Japan.
- **Hinokagatsuchi**—the god of fire; the child of Izanagi and Izanami who caused the death of Izanami.
- **Amaterasu**—the sun goddess, born from Izanagi's left eye.
- **Tsukiyomi**—the god of the moon, born from Izanagi's right eye.
- **Susanoo**—the god of storms, born from Izanagi's nose.

THE CORRECT WAY TO ENTER A SHINTO SHRINE

Instantly recognizable in their beauty and elegance, Shinto shrines are commonplace features of most Japanese landscapes (there are over 80,000 across the country). Built to house communities' various *kami*, they are always adorned with certain necessary features: the *torii* (entrance-gate), the *sando* (a path through the shrine) and the *honden* (where the *kami* themselves are enshrined). Visitors are welcomed in all Shinto shrines, so you can visit one to see these things for yourself. But be aware—certain rituals should be observed:

- Bow once when you enter.
- If you see a water basin, first wash your left hand, then your right, and then finally your mouth.
- At the shrine, bow and clap twice, pray, press your hands together at chest-height and then bow once more.

If you are inclined to contribute to a donation box, bow before you do so, and remember that the 10 and 500 yen coins are believed to be unlucky.

EVEN THE WISHES
OF A SMALL ANT
REACH HEAVEN.

SHINTO PROVERB

Jainism

ORIGIN: *c.*550 BC, India

DEITY: None

SYMBOL: Swastika; Ahimsa

KEY SCRIPTURES: Pravachansara; Kalpa Sutras

MAJOR FIGURE: Mahavira

NOTABLE BRANCHES: Digambara (the sky-clad); Svetambara (the white-clad)

KEY FESTIVALS AND HOLY DAYS: Mahavira Jayanti, March or April (celebrates the birthday of Mahavira); Paryushana, eight days in August or September (a fasting festival)

ESTIMATED ADHERENTS: Approx. 6 million (0.09 percent of world population)

Jainism is similar in many ways to Hinduism and Buddhism: it comes from India; it has been in continuous practice for over 25 centuries; its notion of the afterlife follows the model of reincarnation; and where Hinduism has the enlightenment of *moksha* and Buddhism has *nirvana*, Jainism has *kevala*. Yet, in other ways, it is as distinct from them as it is from other religions, with its own core system of beliefs and practices, and with a history far longer than its official date of origin attests.

BELIEFS

The path to *kevala*—enlightenment—can be found by following the Three Jewels of Jainism:

1. Right perception (the understanding of the true nature of reality)
2. Right knowledge (the process of freeing oneself of doubts about the true nature of reality)
3. Right conduct (the vows, disciplines and ways of life one undertakes along the path)

Unlike the core beliefs of other major religions, there is no mention of god in the Three Jewels. The Jain universe has its heavens and hells, and a divinity of sorts for those who escape the process of rebirth (these are the *jinas*—or "spiritual conquerors"), but the faith has no god in the traditional sense of the word, and instead is often seen as a nontheistic philosophy.

HISTORY

Mahavira (born *c*.599 BC as the Prince Vardhamana) was the founder of Jainism. And yet, at the same time, he was not the first Jain. Instead, he was the twenty-fourth (and most recent) of the tirthankaras: a long line of spiritual teachers reaching back into the haze of ancient history, perhaps for thousands of years, perhaps more. Very little is known about the 23 tirthankaras before Mahavira—in many cases, nothing at all save their names. The first tirthankara was called Rishabhanatha ("Lord Bull"). After him came Ajita ("Invincible One"), and then Shambhava ("Auspicious") and then Abhinandana ("Worship") and so on and so on until the twenty-third tirthankara, Parshvanatha ("Lord Serpent"), who is said to have lived in the ninth century BC, some 250 years before the birth of Mahavira. As a result, Mahavira (who found his own enlightenment by fasting and meditating for 12 years) is often credited not so much with creating Jainism, but with simply curating and refining the teachings of all his predecessors into one coherent philosophy.

THE SWASTIKA

It is a sad fact that the swastika today is remembered as the symbol of Nazism rather than Jainism—two belief systems as different as night and day—and that fact (quite rightly) angers many Jains. The name comes from the Sanskrit word *svastika*, meaning "well-being," and it is a sacred symbol not just in Jainism but in many other eastern religions, including Hinduism and Buddhism. One important distinction to note is that the Nazis only used the clockwise swastika (with the arms bent to the right), whereas Jains use both the clockwise and the anticlockwise (with the arms bent to the left). Therefore, if you see one of the latter, you will know that it is a symbol of spirituality rather than hate.

THE FIVE GREAT VOWS

In order to become a *yati* (Jain monk), the *sadhus* (male) and *sadhvis* (female) must give up all attachments to people, possessions and places in their pursuit of *kevala* by taking the Five Great Vows.

1. *Ahimsa* (non-violence)
2. *Satya* (truth)
3. *Asteya* (non-theft)
4. *Brahmacharya* (celibacy)
5. *Aparigraha* (non-possessiveness)

These Five Vows are absolute. *Yatis* go barefoot so as not to mistakenly step on an insect (and thereby commit violence), cannot touch a member of the opposite sex for fear of arousal, and only eat the (vegetarian, and often vegan) food which is freely offered to them, for even chopping vegetables can be considered an act of violence.

THE LIFE OF LAY JAINS

Of course, Jains who are not monks or nuns are not expected to adhere to the Five Great Vows, and yet the set of rules they are encouraged to follow can still seem fairly strict to non-Jains. Like *yatis*, lay Jains should also practise *ahimsa*, *satya* and *asteya*: they must be vegetarian, they must conduct their business honestly and they must never cheat or steal. However, the rules are relaxed somewhat around sex and possessiveness: lay Jains do not need to practise celibacy, but sex should only be marital and they should even begin to abstain from sex after a son is born; and they do not need to renounce all possessions, though they should possess only what they need to live simply. Meditation is deeply important for lay Jains, and they are expected to meditate for around 48 minutes a day. Similarly, they are encouraged to be respectful and supportive of their *yatis* by giving them food whenever possible, and even by taking on the life of a *yati* for a day.

LIVE AND ALLOW OTHERS TO
LIVE; HURT NO ONE; LIFE IS
DEAR TO ALL LIVING BEINGS.

MAHAVIRA

Baha'i

ORIGIN: 1863, Persia (present-day Iran)

DEITY: God

SYMBOL: Nine-point star

KEY SCRIPTURE: The Kitab-i-Aqdas

MAJOR FIGURE: Baha'ullah

KEY FESTIVAL: Festival of Ridvan, starting on April 20th or 21st (a celebration of Baha'ullah's declaration that he was the Manifestation of God)

ESTIMATED ADHERENTS: Approx. 5 million (0.06 percent of world population)

The youngest of the other major religions, Baha'i celebrated its 150th birthday in 2013. In such a short time, it has succeeded in spreading from its native Iran to a large number of countries around the world, as exemplified by the fact that Baha'i temples can be found on every continent (with the exception of Antarctica). This rapid growth rate is a testament to the inclusiveness of Baha'i—which teaches that all humans are equal in the eyes of God.

BELIEFS

The essential tenets of the Baha'i faith can be broken down into the following:

1. Equality
2. Justice
3. Spiritual oneness

It is this last tenet—the oneness of spirituality—which has made Baha'i so attractive to some and so controversial to others. Within the Baha'i faith, other religions are treated with equal accord. Indeed, though the founder, Baha'ullah, proclaimed himself to be the Manifestation of God, he also proclaimed that he was not the first, and nor would he be the last. Earlier manifestations of God, he said, were Muhammad, Jesus, the Buddha and Moses. The God of whom these people were manifestations is, in the Baha'i faith, one and the same.

HISTORY

Baha'i grew from Babism, a faith founded in Persia by the Shi'ite Muslim Siyyid Ali Muhammad who, in 1844, proclaimed himself to be the "Bab" (literally, the "gate"). His interpretations of the Qur'an and his declaration of prophetic abilities offended the orthodox sensibilities of the authorities, and he was executed. But one of his disciples, Mirza Hoseyn Ali Nuri, took it upon himself to continue and evolve the Bab's work.

In 1863, Mirza Hoseyn Ali Nuri titled himself Baha'ullah: prophet and Manifestation of God. Baha'ullah was dogged by persecution from the moment he founded Baha'i, exiled to Constantinople and later Adrianople, and eventually imprisoned in Acre (in modern-day Israel) for 24 years. Despite all this, his work was so effective that, following his death in 1892, the Baha'i faith continued— and continues—to spread.

UNIVERSAL HOUSE OF JUSTICE

Baha'i has a supreme ruling body known as the Universal House of Justice situated in Haifa, Israel (where the Bab is buried). Composed of nine members who are elected to the position every five years, it guides the evolution of modern Baha'i by ruling on issues not easily solved by the scriptures. One noted peculiarity of the Universal House of Justice is that, despite the declared equality of men and women within the Baha'i faith, women are banned from membership.

PRACTICES

Baha'i has no official clergy or sacraments and the rituals it has (such as marriage) are few. Baha'is believe that the same rituals should not be used by different people from different cultures around the world, for they cannot reflect the rich diversity of these cultures and, indeed, can end up diluting or even destroying this diversity. Nevertheless, despite this lack of clergy, sacraments and rituals, Baha'i is abundant in worship. The fundamental purpose of the faith is to know and to love God. This can be achieved through fasting, meditation and service to others. However, one of the most important ways to know and to love God in Baha'i is through prayer. Baha'ullah made daily prayer obligatory, and one of three particular prayers must be said each day. These are:

- The short prayer (to be recited once between midday and sunset)
- The medium prayer (to be recited once in the morning, once in the afternoon and once in the evening)
- The long prayer (to be recited once at any hour)

Prayer is considered a private duty. Therefore, even during communal worship, there are no congregational prayers. Instead, individuals will recite prayers on behalf of others.

EXECUTION, EXILE AND MURDER

The exile and imprisonment of Baha'ullah—and the execution of his teacher, the Bab, before him—was only the start of the persecution which has long been a part of Baha'i life. In Muslim countries particularly, where followers of Baha'i are often considered apostates from

Islam, their schools have been closed, their cemeteries desecrated and their people murdered. The twenty-first century is no exception to this persecution. In 2016, a Baha'i man was brutally stabbed to death in Iran. When his killers were apprehended, they admitted that they had planned and then carried out his murder because he was a Baha'i.

*"The earth is but one country,
and mankind its citizens."*

BAHA'ULLAH

OTHER SYSTEMS
OF BELIEF

Of course, alongside the major religions so far discussed there are countless other systems of belief spread across the world. These are less well subscribed (with the possible exception of Humanism, adherence to which is difficult to estimate), but no less interesting. Since there is such a diverse range and astonishing number of other systems of belief across the globe, it will come as no surprise that they can't all be covered in this little book. Nevertheless, those which are discussed here are widely known and incredibly fascinating.

Voodoo

ORIGIN: *c.*1600, Americas and the Caribbean

DEITY: Bondye ("the Good God")

SYMBOLS: The *veves* of Agwe, Danbala, Gran Bwa and other spirits

KEY SCRIPTURE: No specific texts, but the Bible is commonly consulted

MAJOR FIGURE: Marie Laveau

KEY FESTIVALS AND HOLY DAYS: Danbala's Saint Day, March 17th (the same as St Patrick's Day); Ogou's Saint Day, July 25th (the same as St James's Day)

NOTABLE BRANCHES: Rada, Daome, Ibo, Nago

ESTIMATED ADHERENTS: Unknown, but some reports claim 60 million people (approx. 0.78 percent of world population) engage in voodoo practices

Voodoo (sometimes known as "Vodou" or "Vodoun," but never "Hoodoo," which is a form of traditional folk magic) is a religion frequently misunderstood and even maligned, often by the medium which represents it the most frequently: Hollywood movies. Forget all the stuff you might have seen featuring human sacrifices, devil worship and black magic—instead, Voodoo is essentially a devotion to the spirits of the universe, known as *Iwa*. Prayer and rituals directed at these spirits ensure good health and fortune for humans (who are spirits themselves: the spirits of the visible world). With its roots in ancient African faiths and heavily influenced by Catholicism, Voodoo is now most commonly practiced in Haiti and parts of North America, including New Orleans.

VOODOO DOLLS

Again, ignore the myths. While dolls are used in some variations of Voodoo, they are never used for the purposes of revenge. It is, rather, the opposite—voodoo dolls, when hung from trees in cemeteries, help people to heal by opening up a line of communication between them and their recently deceased loved ones.

MARIE LAVEAU

BORN: September 10th, 1801, New Orleans

DIED: June 15th 1881, New Orleans (aged 79)

DIED OF: Natural causes

OCCUPATION: Nurse / Hairdresser / Priestess

OTHER NAMES: Voodoo Queen of New Orleans

WHY WAS SHE THE QUEEN? The daughter of a freed slave, Marie Laveau led large (and often theatrical) Voodoo ceremonies across New

134

Orleans. These ceremonies—along with her frequent works of charity, an indomitable personality and rumored magical abilities—built her reputation as a powerful Voodoo priestess, and she regularly received visitors who came to pay their respects or seek her advice.

GRANTER OF WISHES? According to some, yes. Legend has it that if you draw an "X" on her tomb, turn three times, knock on her tomb and then shout your wish, it will be granted.

Rastafarianism

ORIGIN: 1930s, Jamaica

DEITY: Jah

SYMBOLS: Lion of Judah, Flag of Ethiopia

KEY SCRIPTURE: Bible

MAJOR FIGURES: Haile Selassie, Marcus Garvey

KEY FESTIVALS AND HOLY DAYS: Coronation Day, November 2nd (to celebrate the coronation of Haile Selassie as Emperor); Grounation Day, April 21st (marks the day Haile Selassie visited Jamaica)

NOTABLE BRANCHES: Bobo Shanti, Nyabinghi, Twelve Tribes

ESTIMATED ADHERENTS: Approx. 600,000 (0.008 percent of world population)

Rastafarianism (or Rastafari) is a Judeo-Christian religion which began—and today continues most predominantly—in Jamaica. In the 1930s, Jamaican political activist Marcus Garvey prophesied the coming of a black Messiah and claimed that the prophecy was fulfilled when Haile Selassie was crowned Emperor of Ethiopia soon after. Rastafarianism is an inherently political religion, and its interpretations of both the Old and New Testaments focus on the slavery, injustice and oppression suffered by those of African descent. The Book of Exodus, for example, parallels their story of being exiled to Babylon (the Americas, Europe and the Caribbean), while the Book of Revelation predicts their return to Zion (Africa).

"Princes shall come out of Egypt;
Ethiopia shall soon stretch out
her hands unto God."

PSALM 68:31

LIVITY

Rastafarianism was popularized around the world most notably by Bob Marley, and the notions his name conjures—reggae music, dreadlocks and astonishingly large spliffs—are all derived from the Rastafarian lifestyle of "livity."

- **Reggae**—a musical style which grew out of "binghi" ceremonies, featuring drumming through the night.
- **Dreadlocks**—the cutting of hair is forbidden in Rastafarianism, and twisting the long hair into dreads makes it easier to maintain.
- **Marijuana**—abstinence from alcohol is encouraged in Rastafarianism, but the smoking of marijuana is said to enhance spiritual awareness.

HAILE SELASSIE

BORN: July 23rd, 1892, Ejersa Goro, Ethiopia

DIED: August 27th, 1975, Addis Ababa, Ethiopia (aged 83)

DIED OF: Respiratory failure while under house arrest (some claim strangulation by his captors)

WHY WAS HE UNDER HOUSE ARREST? In 1974, following criticism of his leadership in the face of widespread famine and unemployment across Ethiopia, the army deposed Haile Selassie and placed him under house arrest, where he remained for the rest of his life.

OCCUPATION: Emperor of Ethiopia / Messiah

BIRTH NAME: Ras Tafari Makonnen (from which the religion takes its name)

ALSO KNOWN FOR: Famously standing up to the League of Nations against Mussolini's invasion and occupation of Ethiopia.

Modern Paganism

ORIGIN: Highly disputed, but possibly 1967, UK

DEITIES: Thousands—among them Gaia, Brighid, Baldur and Aphrodite

SYMBOLS: Pentacle; Ankh; Triple Moon

KEY FESTIVALS AND HOLY DAYS: Summer Solstice, June 20th, 21st, or 22nd (also known as "Litha"); Winter Solstice, December 21st or 22nd (also known as "Yule")

ESTIMATED ADHERENTS: Approx. 3 million (0.03 percent of world population)

Trying to distill Modern Paganism into one simple, cohesive definition is like trying to explain how a smartphone works in a single text message. So far in this book, we've seen a lot of the inclusive nature of many religions, yet perhaps none is quite as inclusive as Modern Paganism. Worshipped deities range from Celtic to Egyptian to Norse to Greek. Adherents range from Wiccans to Celtic Reconstructionists to Neopagans to Druids. There is no single, absolute way to be a Modern Pagan: it is as fluid and interpretative as nature. And yet that last word is, perhaps, the key to this religion. In essence, Modern Paganism is the reverence of nature. There is, of course, an abundance of other aspects—magic, community, folklore, witchcraft—but the one vital notion which pervades all areas of Modern Paganism is the adoration, and the celebration, of the natural world.

WICCA

Also known as Pagan Witchcraft, Wicca is an eclectic denomination of Modern Paganism, with its own set of varying branches. Most followers prefer the name "Wiccan" to "Witch" as the former is gender-neutral. Wiccans are generally duotheistic, worshipping the Moon Goddess (who represents the feminine side of life) and her consort the Horned God (who represents the masculine).

CELTIC RECONSTRUCTIONISM

Reconstructionism is the idea of practicing a religion from one single culture rather than blending together religions from various cultures (as many other denominations of Modern Paganism do). Celtic Reconstructionists base their religion on the faith and folklore of ancient Celts, adopting their prayers, chants and rituals—such as community celebrations with traditional songs, dances and games.

DRUIDRY

Though Druids may have named themselves after the Celtic Druids of the Iron Age, it is disputed whether they have much in common with them. Modern Druidry is very much nature-centered, and Druids believe that the earth itself is sacred and should be worshipped. Stonehenge is a particularly revered site for Druids, many of whom celebrate the Summer Solstice there.

THE HANDFASTING

Handfastings—increasingly popular ceremonies in the UK—are Modern Pagan weddings. Though the format of the ceremony can change from couple to couple, there are some traditional linchpins of the handfasting which most Modern Pagans adhere to. As the name suggests, the centerpiece of the wedding is the binding of hands with sacred cords. Following this, the couple cement their marriage by jumping over a broom together. While some couples only have one handfasting, it is common for most to have two. The first lasts for one year and one day. If the couple still wants to remain together after this time has passed, they will have another handfasting ceremony, this one lasting for life.

Caodaism

ORIGIN: 1926, French Indochina
(modern-day Vietnam)

DEITY: Cao Dai

SYMBOL: Divine Eye

KEY SCRIPTURES: Prayers of the Heavenly and the
Earthly Way; Divine Path to Eternal Life

MAJOR FIGURE: Ngo Van Chieu

KEY FESTIVALS AND HOLY DAYS: Supreme Being Day,
January or February; Dieu Tri, September or
October (an homage to the Great Mother)

ESTIMATED ADHERENTS: Approx. 5 million
(0.06 percent of world population)

Vietnam's third-largest religion (after Buddhism and Roman
Catholicism), Cao Dai (the name for both the faith and its god)
means "High Tower" or, more metaphorically, "Kingdom of
Heaven." At heart, it teaches that the cycle of reincarnation

can be broken by practices such as prayer, the honor of saints and ancestors, non-violence and vegetarianism, with the Supreme Being (Cao Dai) awaiting the believer in heaven at the end. Its melding of reincarnation and a heavenly god demonstrates just how syncretic Caodaism is: it is influenced by many of the religions we have seen so far in this book—Confucianism, Daoism, Buddhism, Islam and Christianity among them. This openness can also be seen in Caodaism's pantheon of saints, which includes, along with many others, Buddha, Jesus and Confucius, as well as some more surprising additions, such as Julius Caesar, Joan of Arc and Victor Hugo.

THE BIG BANG

In the same way that Caodaism respects and reveres a plethora of other faiths, its syncretic nature even extends to science. Not only is the Big Bang officially recognized in the religion, it is stated that this was the very event which created Cao Dai (the Supreme Being, the one and only god).

Scientology

ORIGIN: 1952, USA

DEITY: Supreme Being

SYMBOL: The Symbol of Scientology (the letter S between the ARC and KRC triangles)

KEY SCRIPTURES: Dianetics: The Original Thesis; Dianetics: The Modern Science of Mental Health; Dianetics: The Evolution of a Science

MAJOR FIGURE: L. Ron Hubbard

KEY FESTIVALS AND HOLY DAYS: L. Ron Hubbard's birthday, March 13th; Formation Day of International Association of Scientologists, October 7th

ESTIMATED ADHERENTS: Approx. 500,000 (0.006 percent of world population)

Scientology's founder, the writer L. Ron Hubbard, coined the name by blending the Latin word *scio* (meaning "to know" or "to understand") with the Greek word *logos* (meaning "word," "reason" or "plan")—therefore, Scientology is defined as the study of knowledge and wisdom. This definition is crucial for Scientologists: while the faith has many of the usual facets of religion (a supreme being, for example), it is more focused upon the ways in which individuals can reach their greatest potential by searching for knowledge of the spiritual self. Often known more for its courting of controversy and the several extremely famous Scientologists (one of whom I don't even need to name—you know who I'm talking about), it is nonetheless a rapidly growing religious movement, with Church of Scientology bases scattered all across the USA. There's even one in Brighton, UK.

KEY WORDS IN SCIENTOLOGY

- Thetan—one's immortal soul, reborn through the process of reincarnation, and infinitely capable.
- Engrams—mental pictures derived from traumas (in one's current and previous lives), which corrupt the thetan.

> Clear—those Scientologists who have succeeded in ridding themselves of all their engrams are called "clear." They are both free from engrams and unable to form any new ones.

The practice of Scientology is less a process of worship and more a course of training (the study of the scriptures) and auditing (spiritual counselling in which one's engrams are cleared). This course, however, does not come cheap. The average cost of the course which gets a Scientologist to the level of "clear" is estimated at over $125,000. And it doesn't stop there. Once the Scientologist reaches "clear," they may then work their way through the eight levels (known collectively as the "Bridge") which lead them toward the attainment of "Operating Thetan" (a state of spiritual awareness not limited by the physical universe) and, finally, "Cleared Thetan Clear" (a state in which the practitioner can essentially create and control their own universe). Each of these levels is increasingly expensive and increasingly secretive: it is said that Level VIII of the

Humanism

Perhaps a little book of world religions is not the right place to discuss Humanism. It is most assuredly not a religion. Indeed, it may not even be a belief. Some choose to call it a "non-belief." Even the word "humanism" is under dispute, with some preferring to lengthen it to "secular humanism" and yet others labelling it under the umbrella term "atheism." You may have noticed that this discrete entry of a religion / belief / philosophy is the only one to open without its key facts. That's because it's near impossible to attribute specific origins or symbols, notable texts or people. And yet Humanism does have its principles, and for this reason it is worth a brief mention, if only as an alternative to all the religions discussed so far.

KEY PRINCIPLES

Humanism strives to move the focus of morality away from the divine and toward the human—there is still a system of ethics in place in the world, it says, but it was created by people, and it is people who continue to maintain it. The

Bridge (a level called "The Truth Revealed") tells the practitioner the ultimate truth of who they really are, and is so confidential that it is only delivered on board MV *Freewinds*, the church's private cruise ship.

L. RON HUBBARD

BORN: March 13th, 1911, Nebraska, USA

DIED: January 24th, 1986, California, USA (aged 74)

DIED OF: Stroke

FINAL YEARS: Spent as a recluse living in a motorhome

OCCUPATION: Founder of the Church of Scientology / Author (predominantly science fiction/fantasy)

WHAT DOES THE L STAND FOR? Lafayette

needs of humans are central, and the value of human life is the focus of all ethical concerns. Within Humanism, people can still follow the Golden Rule, can still treat others as they wish to be treated themselves, and can do so without any need of the divine or supernatural.

BELIEFS AND PRACTICES

Myriad as they are, let's focus on the beliefs and practices of the two most notable branches of Humanism.

RELIGIOUS HUMANISM

This branch can be referred to as a nontheistic religion. Maintaining the key belief of the overall movement (that the needs of humans are central), Religious Humanism combines this with rituals and ideas more commonly seen in places of worship. Weddings, funerals and many other congregational practices, for example, can involve numerous aspects of their religious counterparts and remain distinctly Humanist. The beliefs and practices of Religious Humanism can be broken down into yet further subdivisions: Humanistic Judaism encourages secular

Jewish people to embrace their culture and identity rather than the faith itself and take part in Jewish holidays and celebrations; Christian Humanism uses the teachings of Jesus to highlight the importance of kindness and happiness.

SECULAR HUMANISM

While Secular Humanism is naturalistic (meaning that they believe there is no supernatural, and that only the natural world exists), it does not outright reject and dismiss religion, but instead takes a more comprehensive worldview. A Secular Humanist society is one where all people, regardless of their religious or non-religious beliefs, are equal, and should be treated as such. The idea of State Secularism follows this definition, and there are currently 96 officially secular states around the world. One of the fundamental tenets of Secular Humanism is that of inquiry—we should accept nothing based purely on blind faith, but should comprehensively examine any ideology we are presented with in a scientific and philosophical manner.

Conclusion

There we have it. Perhaps not religion in a nutshell, but religion in a little book at least. And the purpose of it all was never to inculcate, but rather to inform. Never to proselytize, but to explain. Never to foist—and never even to defend—religion, but to describe, and to recount, and to foster knowledge and understanding of the many faiths which filter through all our lives, no matter what we choose to believe or how we choose to identify. Religion is a rich tapestry, filled with beautifully told stories, notions of delight and insight, and answers to questions we all at some point in our lives ask ourselves. They might not be the right answers, and they might not be the wrong answers either, but they serve to illuminate the human condition nonetheless.

THE PERSECUTION OF THE NON-RELIGIOUS

In ages and countries where religion has dominated public thought, those who have stood apart from the majority and professed their non-belief in any particular dogma or ideology have often come under attack. During the Spanish Inquisition, for example, atheists were frequently targeted for torture or execution. It is a pattern which continues to this day, not just for atheists, but for those who identify as Humanist too. A recent report shows that, in 2017, Humanists were actively persecuted in seven countries (with instances including violence and murder) and faced severe discrimination in a further 78 countries.

Ultimately, this book's primary aim is for you to have learned a thing or two about the world's many religions which you didn't know before. Should you desire to learn more, I wish you nothing but the best—for surely our greater understanding of religion, allied to greater tolerance and freedom of worship across the globe, whether we subscribe to a particular religion or not, will make this world a better place. Because, at its core, an understanding of religion leads to a greater understanding of people. That's something we can all believe in.

The
LITTLE BOOK OF
PHILOSOPHY

Rachel Poulton

IMAGE CREDITS

THE LITTLE BOOK OF
PHILOSOPHY

Rachel Poulton

$13.95
Paperback
ISBN: 978-1-63228-077-0

If you want to know your Socrates from your Sartre and your Confucius from your Kant, this approachable little book will introduce you to the key thinkers, themes and theories you need to know to understand how human ideas have sculpted the world we live in and the way we think today.